SmartScale™ Playbook

Business Accelerator for Mid-Life Companies

An Important Note:

This workbook is supplemental and is not a "stand alone manual or book."

The SmartScale™ Workbook was designed to lead you through the implementation of SmartScale™ and maximize your successful application of the tools, concepts and methodologies as experienced in the sessions.

To stay current on the latest SmartScaling insights – and to join the ScaleWerks™ Community visit scalewerks.co

All content contained in this e-book is proprietary. Duplication in any form, in whole or in part, is not permitted without the authors' written authorization.

Contributing Authors: Jake Cook, Mark Jacobs, Ron Malone, Kenneth May

Copyright 2018 Mark Jacobs, Ron Malone and Ken May ALL RIGHT RESERVED

Version control: MASTER – 11-28-18, XL

TABLE OF CONTENTS

What is SmartScale™? 4

    An Answer for Midlife Companies That Want to Rapidly Increase Equity Value 4

    The ScaleWerks™ Protocol 5

Getting Started 8

SmartScale™ Lab 12

    What Jobs are Your Customers Hiring You to Do?..............12

    Business Purpose 18

SmartScale™ 24

Accelerator 24

    1.   Define or Create Your Business Model 24

    2.   Assess Current Customer Base 30

    3.   Define Your Category 33

    4.   Claim and Affirm Your Authority 36

    5.   Design Your Community 40

    6.   Design Platform 45

    7.   Prioritize Key Processes and Set Objectives 47

    8.   Create Master Program of Projects 50

    9.   GoForward 51

IMPLEMENT 52

Tools and Methodologies 52

Immunity to Change 55

....58

Employee Engagement 59

Glossary...65

Bibliography 59

What is SmartScale™?

An Answer for Midlife Companies That Want to Rapidly Increase Equity Value

Scaling is about adding revenue at an exponential rate while only adding resources at an incremental rate.

We define scale as two complementary components:

- Exponential Growth where revenue per customer (which we re-define as "community member") increases as the size of the community grows, while

- Achieving Economies of Scale (proportionate reduction in costs per dollar of revenue gained by an increased level of sales)

From our point of view, when a company is scaling it exhibits these seven dimensions:

1. Unit costs decline as it grows.

2. Product or service value grows as sales increase.

3. Service costs decrease.

4. Category dominance and rapidly increasing sales from customer recognition of the company as the authority in the category.

5. Operational costs decline as a percentage of revenue.

6. Innovation is an integral part of the culture.

7. Shared values and expectations as expressed through a structured measurement and feedback process.

The ScaleWerks ™ Protocol

The ScaleWerks™ curve demonstrates the exponential growth ("Scale") created through our Protocol of Transforming the Customer Base while Lifting Revenue per Customer.

The "Y" – **Transform the Customer Base** – axis is a powerful, deep-insight, deep-relationship continuum.

The base of the continuum is grounded in knowing your audience. With deep-insight analytics you gain a granular level understanding of your audience – enabling you to clearly define the jobs that your audience comes to you to have done.

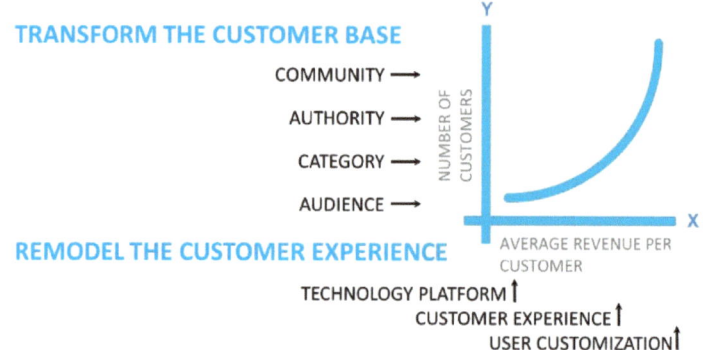

1. With a clear, data supported understanding of those jobs you can define your product and service offerings from a whole new perspective – not a niche or market competitor – but a category leader.
2. To be a category leader you MUST become the Authority in the jobs that customers come to you to have done. Being the Authority means engaging, educating, and attracting your audience into a community that's built around the category that you lead.

The "X" axis – **Remodel the Customer Experience** – is built on capabilities that provide value to your customers:

1. A customer-centric technology platform that facilitates fast, intuitive and engaging interfaces, collects relevant information and organizes it to support efficient, intelligent decision processes by both the customer and the company.
2. A smart customer experience which makes it a pleasure for your customers to interact with you to collect information and execute transactions.
3. The ability to leverage precise customer insights, generated from your data, that empowers you to quickly customize your interactions, products, product mix and service to meet the "wants" of your customers…and leave them with a "Wow!"

The X and Y axis work together to generate scale.

As you increase or expand your customers' capacities to do the job they want to have done, the more they tell other potential customers about the positive experience. This causes growth to accelerate because it follows the laws of the network effect.

As the size of the community grows, the more valuable it becomes. As the authority that leads the community, you can use the data collected to identify more opportunities to service the wants of your community.

As you identify more opportunities to satisfy community member wants, you scale. As you scale you're presented with the opportunity to evolve your business model.

GETTING STARTED
Are We Able to Scale?

If you've run a company over an extended period then you've experienced periods when sales growth slows, profit margins get squeezed, or return on assets in general decreases. Typically, our first reaction is to work harder – until we recognize that additional effort provides no additional return.

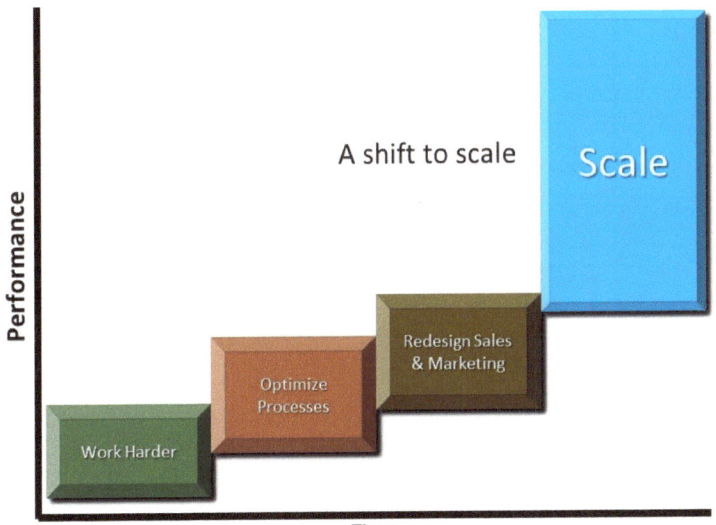

Since working harder didn't provide marginal return we decide to work smarter. We'll try to optimize the operations of the business to increase profit margins. Optimization programs can deliver meaningful results, but over time those efforts meet with marginal returns on the time invested. Assuming our optimization processes are successful, we enjoy short-term cost, quality and efficiencies that we can use to change our pricing strategy; which in turn inspires us to redesign our sales and marketing efforts. However, those sales and marketing efforts also are doomed to marginal returns as our competitors recognize our efforts and match them.

Realizing that our product sales and marketing efforts don't deliver transformative performance gains - and recognizing that these efforts are nothing more than adjustments in our current business model - we come to grips with the hard truth that our effort must be placed into rethinking the *entire* business model. And here's where it gets hard.

For many executives changing the business model means acquiring new divisions, new product lines, or changing the go-to-market strategy. At their core, these tactical maneuvers simply continue the existing business model, with add-ons that are mere extensions of the core business.

In order to have a meaningful impact on earnings and growth, the business model needs to be transformed.

According to Bain and Company, depending on the industry, each dollar in additional sales volume is worth six times more to the valuation of the business than each dollar saved through process optimization. Now, imagine combining both rapid sales growth with the benefits of process optimization; and the valuation increase a business that achieves both sales escalation and cost optimization would realize. That company would be scaling if it is rapidly adding customers at the same time that it's increasing the value of each customer.

> *Only by forcing our brains to recategorize information and move beyond our habitual thinking patterns can we begin to imagine truly novel alternatives.*

Achieving scale can't be done with the traditional business model. Traditional business models can support rapid growth, but not scale.

The SmartScale™ Lab is the first step to answer the question - Will your business scale?

SmartScale™ Lab Agenda

1. Define Scale
2. What jobs people want done, when they buy from you?
   a. Job(s) to be Done Analysis
   b. Understand what the market wants (vs needs)
   c. What difference do you make? (From/To)
   d. Business Purpose
   e. Customer avatars
3. Schedule a post SmartScale™ Lab follow-up conference call.
   a. Decide if the company has a basis upon which to scale.

Next Steps

Schedule post-lab follow-up to discuss if company has a basis upon which to scale. The follow up discussion topics:

1. Based on the discussions during the SmartScale Lab, are you an authority on accomplishing the job your company does (or could be doing)?
    a. As the Authority do you (or could you) do the job differently enough that the audience sees the approach as a preferred product/process/experience?
    b. As an Authority are you attracting (can you attract) an audience?
2. Can the current (or future) product/process/experience grow enough in value over time that users will stay engaged in order to get more value from the product/process/experience?
    a. How are you measuring customer value today?
3. What's the estimated value of the market, as defined by the job that your company gets (or could be getting) hired to do.
4. Does your organization want to scale around its Authority?

If the follow up meeting ends in mutual agreement that there is a scalable business model, the next step is the 8-week Accelerator. This is a collaborative process utilizing internal databases, financial modelling, input from employees, and customer analysis. The Accelerator concludes with a Go Forward plan from which your company can scale.

SmartScale™ Elements

SmartScale™ Lab

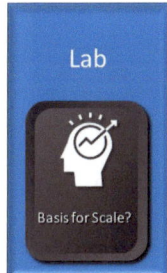

What Jobs are Your Customers Hiring You to Do?

Eliminate their struggles – you get hired.

The central idea behind Jobs Theory is, "your customers are not buying your products or services; they're hiring them to get a job done." If you understand what that job is, you can identify what causes customers to hire your products.

This process is designed to find unmet wants by helping you precisely articulate and quantify your customers' struggles. A want is unmet if:

1. It has high importance and the customer is currently struggling with low satisfaction.
2. The job executor wants something to happen quickly or accurately but cannot make it happen with their current solution.

When you identify a want that is important to your customer, they will be primed to switch to your solution.

An important benefit of this process is that messaging based on satisfying the job-to-be-done is easy for customers to understand. And because the wants in the job-to-be-done are prioritized based on importance and satisfaction, you can create messages that speak clearly to your authority to satisfy the customers' wants...and position yourself as the Category Leader.

Defining the Job

Define the Core Function of the JTBD		Define Outcomes	Define Emotional Job
When Trying To...	It is difficult to...	People struggle to...	And want to feel and be perceived as...
When trying to accomplish...	It is difficult to do because the process	What makes getting this job done time consuming, inefficient, unpredictable, inconvenient or difficult?	When getting this job done, how do you want to be perceived by others and how do you want to feel or avoid feeling?

Wants vs. Needs

What "wants" resonate with your customers?

This is always a tough one: what is it that my customers want vs what they need?

To help you think about this we've divided Wants into three categories – Power, Achievement, and Affiliation.

Start with those categories, then in the Customer Needs column write out what has to happen in order for your customer to achieve each of the items listed under these three categories of Wants. If you get stuck, we'll work on this in our coaching session.

	Customer Wants	Customer Needs
Power		
Achievement		
Affiliation		

You Make a Difference

What are you saving people "from" – and taking them "to"?

Ok – so people recognize you as an Authority – a Category Leader. They use what you offer to rock their world and are delighted that they hired you. What's that really mean? What's it like for them before they found you? What's it like now that they made the big step and are actively engaged?

Use this worksheet to tell their "now" story, and the glory that they will experience once they join up and become active participants/users.

- What do they have now? What will they get?
- What it feels like now – without you? What's the feeling they have once they are all in and can't live without you?
- What's their day like now? How awesome is it going to be once they're an avid, committed, consistent participant and user?
- How will their status change in the eyes of their customers and friends?
- What Wants - or Ghosts – does this resonate with?
    - Power
    - Achievement
    - Affiliation

Follow the filter through – filling in lines until you get stuck...then move to the next group.

From – To Grids

Have and Have Not's

	From: Before You Came Along	To: Now That They Are A Member of Your Community	Does this appeal to Power, Achievement or Affiliation?
1			
2			
3			
4			
5			

Feel

	From: Before You Came Along	To: Now That They Are A Member of Your Community	Does this appeal to Power, Achievement or Affiliation?
1			
2			
3			
4			
5			

Average Day

	From: Before You Came Along	To: Now That They Are A Member of Your Community	Does this appeal to Power, Achievement or Affiliation?
1			
2			
3			
4			
5			

Status

	From: Before You Came Along	To: Now That They Are A Member of Your Community	Does this appeal to Power, Achievement or Affiliation?
1			
2			
3			
4			
5			

Business Purpose

If you don't stand for something, you'll fall for anything.

If you're not focused on helping people and doing something spectacular what's the point of your business being in the market?

Use this worksheet to define the undeniable, driving purpose behind your business. Read the story – and answer the questions that follow.

This is a visualization exercise. After you read this, close your eyes for a minute and imagine yourself 5 years from now.

Imagine that you're in an auditorium in which someone is speaking and announcing an award. You realize that the person speaking is someone you admire deeply, and the award is for having significantly enhanced the lives and well-being of the members of your community. The presenter says, 'This award is in appreciation for all you have enabled us, as members of the community that you designed and built, to accomplish for ourselves and those around us.' There is a standing ovation as people go wild with cheering and applaud.

When the applause dies down the presenter goes on to list all the accomplishments that your community members have achieved. Listen to what the presenter is saying *(take a minute – and close your eyes to think about this question)*. What was it that was accomplished?

```
┌─────────────────────────────────────────┐
│                                         │
│                                         │
│                                         │
│                                         │
└─────────────────────────────────────────┘
```

A video starts. There is a group of community members in a discussion, and one community member says, 'The thing that is great about this organization is...' *(Take a minute – and close your eyes to think about this)*. Fill it in...what did that community member say?

```
┌─────────────────────────────────────────┐
│                                         │
│                                         │
│                                         │
│                                         │
└─────────────────────────────────────────┘
```

Other jumps in, 'That's all fine and wonderful, but the thing that really makes being a member of this community stand out is...' *(Take a minute – and close your eyes to think about this)*.

```
┌─────────────────────────────────────────┐
│                                         │
│                                         │
│                                         │
│                                         │
└─────────────────────────────────────────┘
```

You get up to accept the award and explain that five years before a group came together to develop a plan that has resulted in this award. You explain several things that were done. *(Take a minute – and close your eyes to think about this)*....What was it that the organization did?

```
┌─────────────────────────────────────────┐
│                                         │
│                                         │
│                                         │
│                                         │
└─────────────────────────────────────────┘
```

As you are leaving you overhear a group of employees talking. They are saying that they didn't believe the organization could actually design the Community and grow it, but that it did. They begin talking about what it feels like to be a part of the organization and how the experience has changed/improved their lives. Listen to what they are saying. How does it feel to work there? *(Take a minute – and close your eyes to think about this).*

Customer Avatar

Jenny is the perfect customer. So, who is she…EXACTLY? Here's your chance to nail that down.

If you're not focused on helping the right people, you'll waste tons of time and money. You don't want bad customers, and you don't want to fool around with people who will never become customers.

Use this worksheet to build a definition of the perfect customer. It's important that you think of this customer as a student – willing to learn, experiment and trust…because that's how we are going to build your community – by attracting people who want to learn, experiment, trust and succeed. Here's the formula we'll use –

Physical description + what they want + their biggest problem + how they buy + best way to engage with them.

Pro-tip: You are not going to sell the know-it-all, old hack or resistor to change…so imagine the perfect student of your product or industry…and forget the scrubs.

This should only take 20 mins.

The AVATAR example:

Jenny

Jenny is the CEO of a mid-life specialty foods company located in the United States. She wants a practical game plan to grow her business.

Jenny's company sells to busy professionals who travel and are interested in eating healthily at layovers or between meals.

Jenny's problem is that she understands her customer's pain better than anyone, but she has not been able to grow the business more that 10% per year for the past 5 years.

Jenny buys after a face to face. She's happy with monthly retainers but prefers revenue shares. She chooses vendors mainly through introductions from trusted advisers. She values her professional networks and takes time to check out anyone who is referred to her.

What is the perfect individual's physical description?

What does the perfect individual want?

What is the perfect individual's biggest problem?

What is the best way to engage with the perfect individual?

What are they For?

What are they Against?

What do they Want?

What do they Fear?

SmartScale™

Accelerator

1. Define or Create Your Business Model

Groundwork: Four Business Models

Based on your customer knowledge and business design, you have four business model options. (See Weil and Woemner illustration, below.)

	Business Design based on Value Chain	Business Design based on Ecosystem
Expansive, complete customer knowledge	**3. Omnichannel** • Seamless customer experience with access to many products across many channels (physical stores, websites, mobile apps, etc.) • "Own" the customer relationship • Customer selects channels • Advanced & seamless supply chain • Shares data between channels • Personalized brand messaging	**4. Ecosystem** • Becomes the "go-to" source • Active community with effective member interactions • Collects and reacts well to deep, rich customer data to ensure customer has "great" experience • Can offer broad product offering • Platform owner's revenue is based on transactions
Some or little customer knowledge	**1. Supplier** • Sell their products & services through other companies • Not in a position to command market power • Compete on price • Innovation is incremental • Linear value chain model • Low agility capabilities	**2. Modular Producer** • Plug-and-play product/service • Able to adapt to any ecosystem • Constant innovation of product/service • Must be among the best in their category • Highly competitive market with little customer loyalty

Graphic based on P. Weill and S.L. Woerner, "Thriving in an Increasingly Digital Ecosystem," MIT Sloan Management Review

The greatest opportunity in our "Information Era" for a company to scale is by creating value in ecosystems ("*Ecosystem Communities*") rather than in value chains.

The least likely quadrant for scaling is *Supplier*. However, all four quadrants are viable routes to success, provided you are clear on what your overall strategy is and what that strategy requires to be a Category Leader.

Suppliers have little or no knowledge of the preferences of their end customers. They probably do not have a direct relationship with them. They sell their products and services to distributors in the value chain. Because product information is easily found on the internet, they are vulnerable to pricing pressures and commoditization. Washing machine manufacturers are a good example of Suppliers.

Modular Producers are providers of products and services (like payments) that work with any ecosystem. Their plug-and-play offerings can work with any number of channels or partners. They depend on others for distribution and for guidance on what the customer needs. Payment companies are good examples. They enable the consumer to pay for a wide range of goods and services.

If you are a Modular Producer, you need to be great at about everything because competition is fierce. Customers choose you based on innovation and price.

Omnichannel Businesses have deep knowledge of their customers because of their direct relationship with them. This knowledge is essential for building out an integrated customer experience. By providing customers access to their products in various digital and physical channels, it offers a seamless experience that will retain and attract consumers. Many banks, some retailers, and insurance companies are an Omnichannel. IKEA is a good example.

Ecosystem (Community) have a deep end-customer knowledge, and a broad supply base. They leverage these dimensions to provide customers with a seamless experience, selling not only their own proprietary products and services but also those from providers across the entire ecosystem. Thus, they create value for themselves while extracting rent from others. Large internet retailers in the U.S. and China are good examples of Ecosystem Drivers, as are some healthcare providers.

Knowing which business model describes you today – and which business model you aspire to – are instructive to your SmartScale™ efforts.

Based on the Model Description, Answer Two Questions:

Which quadrant do I fall into today?
_____

Which one, if any, should I move to?
_____

The Assessment will identify your capability gaps, based on our Scaling Capability Canvas:

The Scaling Canvas is a template for scaling your business. We will identify and analyze the gaps between current capabilities and those necessary to achieve scale. To make the process simple and actionable we focus on core protocols and enablers.

The core protocol is shown in the diagram below – and labeled as the SmartScale™ Protocol.

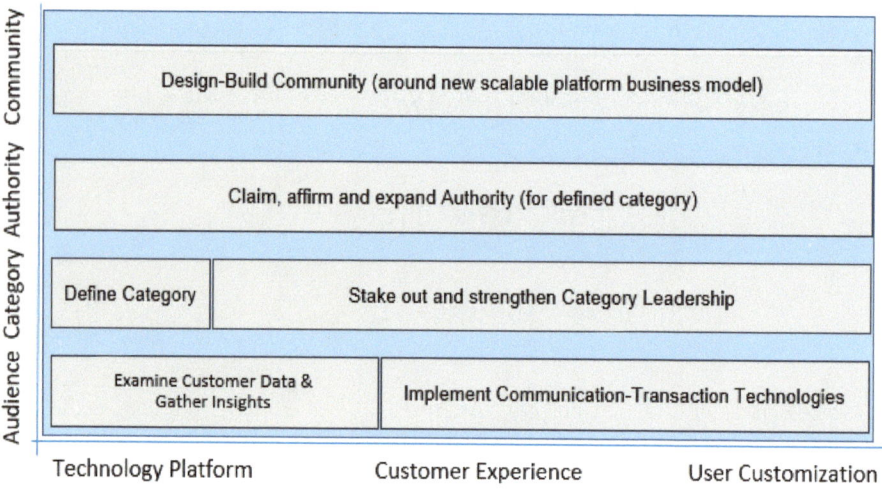

The enablers are what you use to make the core protocols happen. If your enablers don't support the protocols effectively, you won't be able to scale.

We use the following questions to help identify and prioritize the gaps you need to address in your implementation plan:

- What capabilities do you have today compared to the capabilities you need?
- How can you leverage your current capabilities?
- What capabilities should you shed?
- What competencies do your employees need?

We'll build scorecards with performance metrics that establish baselines, support processes that guide achievement of the plan, and monitor improvement.

The outcomes from this work will be the creation of a business which will dominate your category and scale.

Why financial modeling is important.

As you build and implement your firm's game-changing SmartScale™ map you'll need reliable, timely and relevant measures to help you analyze the impact of decisions and provide dashboards to guide activities.

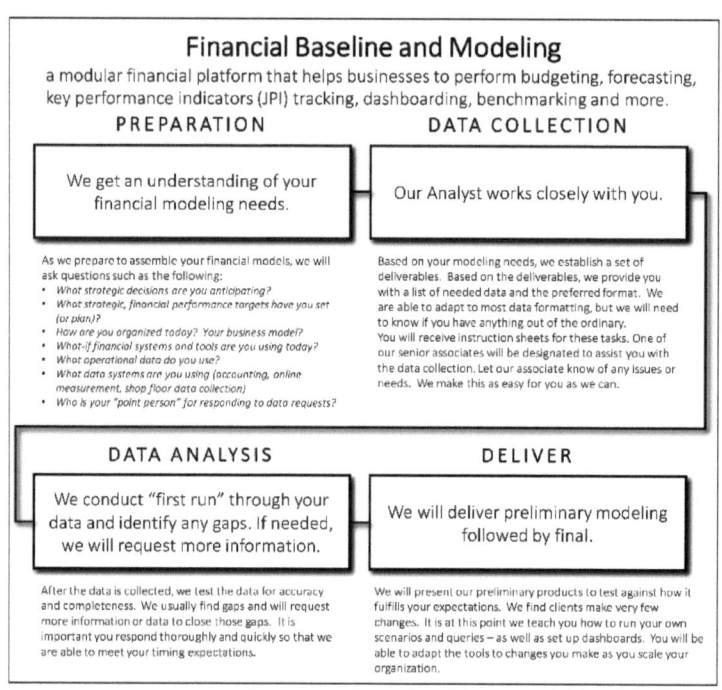

OnPlan, delivers financial modeling expertise and an intuitive system that combines activity-based measurement with financial reporting. The output is smart, real-time, integrated dashboards that enable insightful strategic analysis, tactical planning, financial decision making and implementation feedback for you and your team.

2. Assess Current Customer Base

Know Your Audience

Data Science Is The Key To Marketing ROI - Companies that scale are built on top of customer centricity and the marketing data that drives with it.

> According to Greylock's Josh Elman, "The best growth teams identify the core insights that get users from 'curious' to 'activated habitual' users and build every feature and program in the product—including the nonsoftware features that are a part of the whole product—to get users through this hurdle faster.

SmartScaling requires reliable, predictive and prescriptive insights into your audience. Working with TadPull you'll gain deep insight through advanced statistical services, methods, modeling, and machine learning resources. We unite that deep insight with creative work to go past the tactics of traditional digital marketing and into a space where you can see a payoff today; and unleash a customer experience that delivers sustainable scale.

Tadpull has developed a patent-pending framework that helps manage all your online customer touch points in an integrated way across SEO, Paid & Social Media and Email. Over time, this 1:1 layer of customer data allows you to use data science tactics to predict key metrics like customer lifetime value, propensity to churn, and customer wants. This deep insight is critical to SmartScaling your business.

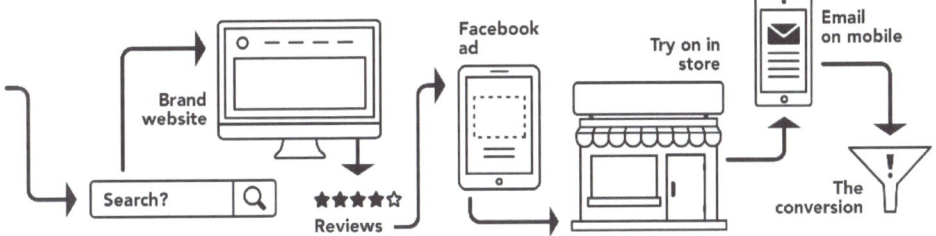

The messy customer journey across devices and channels (Image courtesy of Tadpull).

The brands of tomorrow are being built on remarkable customer experiences today. Tadpull believes every company will have to navigate the digital experience as companies like Amazon and Uber forever change what we all expect in a frictionless digital consumer experience.

The first step on the journey is to recognize that it is a journey. Building on the power of the SmartScaling framework, companies start with framing out the cultural components at the leadership level for implementing change, all the while knowing that it requires a new way of thinking as an organization. This directive has to start at the top and with a core belief that technology and data will help fuel the customer insights for scaling with technology.

To start this journey, Tadpull begins with a qualitative study of your best customers by conducting an in-depth interview and synthesis process to understand how your brand is being perceived today, where the opportunities lie, ideal digital experiences your customers expect and how competitors are encroaching on your marketshare. These insights are collapsed down into key metrics across the user journey and leveraged to guide all marketing campaign work across creative, content, device and timing.

In conjunction, Tadpull's data science team builds custom attribution and acquisition models based on the data available to predict customer lifetime value. This becomes the north star for applying the real-time math around customer acquisition and retention (which is sadly often overlooked and also helps with evaluating which marketing tactics produce the highest ROI). These custom models take into account a variety of different dimensions around your customer including purchase history, frequency, recency, and behavioral engagement across your digital channels.

With this foundation in place, the Tadpull Pond™ software is implemented on your web property to create, manage, and automate all online campaigns across SEO, Social, Paid and Email with the added benefit of allowing you to track individual site behavior and also capture a Net Promoter Score (NPS) on a 1:1 level. Over time, this dataset becomes a critical asset in your business as you can build and eventually automate highly targeted segments. In addition, the software let's you catch issues in real-time such as high acquisition costs, disgruntled customers, website problems and poor performing marketing campaigns.

If your business runs on inventory, the software will also start to identify optimization opportunities for cross-selling and upselling based on individual behavior and past-purchases. An added benefit is unifying Operations and Marketing, so your team is driving campaigns based on what's in stock and more importantly what's most profitable in your inventory mix.

Companies leveraging this customer-first approach with a cross-channel methology tend to see increases of 5-40% for top-line revenue growth that compounds on an annual basis. Based on the framework and results for its clients.

Tadpull was recently named to CIOReview's Top 20 Digital Marketing Solution Providers in 2018 and was the first company globally to be selected by Oracle NetSuite for its commerce agency program with the distinction for digital strategy and user experience.

3. Define Your Category

Category

A scaling strategy centers on category leadership. It's built on:

1. A clear definition of the job that your audience wants to have done (aka "Category"),
2. Leading the unique category as the authority ("Category King") on getting that job accomplished.

SmartScale™ Axiom: To achieve scale you must create a category in which competitors are weaker or irrelevant

Creating a new category involves:

- The active, clear understanding of customers' wants (aspirations) – even if they can't clearly see the want themselves!
- A simple, clearly articulated category definition that tells the audience what job you do for them. That definition, when first heard by the
- Customer must unleash an Aha! Moment.

Why a Category?

"Category Kings," defined as market-share leaders in specific business sectors, often wind up creating the majority of the market value relative to their competition.

Category Kings are market-dominating companies that give us new ways of living, thinking, or doing business, often solving problems we didn't know we had. They become authorities by identifying and then solving these problems. As authorities they earn the right to create and lead a community of practice around the new way of living. These

Category Kings earn **76%** of the market cap of their space.

© Play Bigger TTMC Research 2014

companies end up owning more than 76% of their category's market valuation, with other companies in their space fighting over the scraps.

Category Kings reinvent the status quo. They tell a story that says, "We're not a business, we're a movement. Come join us."

The movement, when properly architected, results in communities of practice. These communities of practice, at their core, capitalize on Metcalfe's law (referred to as the network effect). The network effect leads to more efficient sales and marketing activity; creates strong barriers to competition; delivers explosive growth as a Category King's base of users grows; opens the door to the opportunity to change the business model from "pipeline" to "platform".

Define Your Category

> Use the work and output from the workbook and SmartScale™ Lab to define your category (Include "Job to Be Done" sections).

Name Your Category

Category names anchor you to the problem you solve. They help people understand what you deliver. They set expectations about how you fit into their life experience. When a category name resonates, it anchors a meaningful connection with people.

When defining a new category, it's tempting to come up with a catchy, quirky, "make a mark" category name. But don't fall for that. Names that aren't easily recognizable create confusion and will get "so what" reactions from your audience. You need a category name that people understand and "get" without explanation.

Simplicity is Key. Choose a name that's simple and recognizable. There are a few ways to go about it:

- A Few Known Words: Credit Card, Data Center, Sports Drink, Cloud-based CRM, Safest Car Available, Muscle Shock Strength Building
- Compound Name: Automobile, Bicycle, Laptop
- Derive a New Word from an Existing Word: Browser, E-commerce

Category Name Chosen from Brainstorming and Confirming Research:

4. Claim and Affirm Your Authority

Authority Map Introduction

What does it mean to be an Authority?

An authority is:

1. Recognized as the expert in the job-to-be-done and respected for what they stand for as a business and individual.

2. Helpful to people by creating expert content that's specific to the wants of the target audience and guides them to solve problems.

3. Trusted.

Being an authority isn't about how many Twitter followers or Facebook likes you have. It's not about how much web traffic you get. Real authorities solve their audience's problems. Consistently. Repeatedly. That's why people listen to them. And spread their ideas.

Authority Map

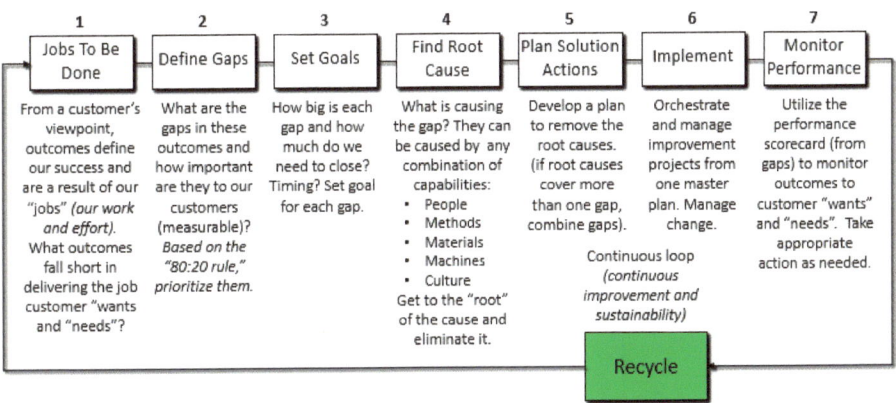

- What problems is your audience experiencing?

- Why are they experiencing that problem?

- What solutions will we offer including content, learning blasts and experiences?

- How, when and where do we deliver those experiences?

Authority Action Plan Participant Activity

Action Planning Worksheet

Audience	Customers of our oil change stores			
Jobs To Be Done	The audiences want us to take care of car maintenance. They pay to have their oil changed, filter changed in at a fair costs. They will pay as a convenience for other maintenance "add-ons" (i.e., wiper blades, air filters). Some audiences buy car-related items on display if a "deal".			
Define Gaps (Problems)	Customers' have no or little knowledge of our minor maintenance services beyond oil & filters	When customers pay, they are surprised to see a higher price for add-on's.	Associates provide poor estimates for add-on on products and services	
Measurable Goal For Closing Gap	Increase revenue, by store, for "other" products and services.	Increase revenue, by store, for add-on products and services.	Improve customer satisfaction survey results relating to add-on's from "poor" to "excellent"	
Root Causes (Actionable)	No knowledge of product offerings across all 26 stores and not listed in register computers. No internal or external store marketing.	Pricing inconsistency on store add-on's. Price higher than DIY.	Associates are incentivized to sell add-ons with bonuses.	
Solution Actions & Estimated Completion Date	Create a company-wide product and service offering to include ongoing product development	March 31 2019		
Solution Actions & Estimated Completion Date	Develop and execute company-wide employee education and awareness program (include ongoing refresh)	June 10 2019		
Solution Actions & Estimated Completion Date	Develop marketing program for markets and in-store (signage, hand out, employee scripting)	July 2 2019		
Solution Actions & Estimated Completion Date	Develop store-level scorecard to monitor sales of "other" product and services	July 2 2019		
Solution Actions & Estimated Completion Date	Institute (customer and employee friendly) ordering and payment system with POS information to corporate offices.			

Authority Action Planning Worksheet

Action Planning Worksheet										
Audience	Jobs To Be Done	Define Gaps (Problems)	Measurable Goal For Closing Gap	Root Causes (Actionable)	Solution Actions & Estimated Completion Date	Solution Actions & Estimated Completion Date	Solution Actions & Estimated Completion Date	Solution Actions & Estimated Completion Date	Solution Actions & Estimated Completion Date

5. Design Your Community

Community Map Introduction

"A community may begin as an online gathering, but in order to truly flourish it will have to put down roots in the offline world too." · *21 Lessons for the 21st Century, by Yuval Noah Harari*

Community Implementation Map

Phase	Base-line Deliverables	Action Steps
Getting started.	Purpose Statement. Measurable Outcomes/Goals. An Executive Sponsor. Team Members.	
Community Design - Research. Connecting customer wants to community purpose.	Clear definition and confirmation of the value to community members through interviews, surveys, data analysis, trends and a description of: (1) what it looks like to participate in the community and (2) a clear statement of the value that community membership provides.	
Architecting the strategic plan and measurement framework. Developing, short and long-term strategic plans, goals and measurement processes.	Prioritized list of the value that community will provide to community members. Identification of community-centric activities based on the top 4-5 value items. Definition of measurable outcomes from each of the community-centric activities.	

Community Implementation Map, Continued

Phase	Base-line Deliverables	Action Steps/Due Date
Test and adjust.	Execution of limited-sized events to test community-centric activities. Evaluation of each event based on pre-defined measurable outcomes. Re-run of events if necessary to adjust or improve.	
Executing Community Growth Strategy.	Build/update tactical roll-out plans based on test results.	
Continuous Improvement.	Develop and implement continuous feedback and community governance processes that insure that the community is meeting member expectations, contributing to the company's category leadership standing, achieving target outcomes and growing	

Customer Experience Tool

Use Customer Experience Tool to:

- Understand customers' goals and what leaves them satisfied or frustrated
- Identify gaps between what a business thinks it is delivering and what a customer actually experiences
- Improve customer relationships with the company
- Enable mangers to run their businesses around customer episodes (namely, interactions such as paying a bill or researching a purchase) rather than around internal organizational silos (such as managing the help desk or accounts payable)
- Gain insights into which sequence of events leads a customer to a positive result or an unsatisfactory one
- Reduce customer complaints and turnover rates
- Define successful performance
- Increase performance first by doing well what customers value most and then by linking each step of the experience in order to make it feel seamless and easy to navigate
- Cut costs by decreasing waste, cycle times and time to market

What the Customer Experience Tool does:

- Analyzes all steps and aspects of customer interactions
- Combines data about each interaction with information about the impact on customer satisfaction, loyalty and business economics
- Connects performance metrics previously held by separate business units to illuminate how a customer experiences a service from start to finish
- Better interprets data from a customer's experience by connecting pieces to each other and to customers' perceptions of value
- Illuminates where there is waste in the journey—waste of customers' time and of company resources—especially across distribution channels, revealing opportunities to reduce the cost of serving customers while also improving the customer experience

Customer Experience Worksheet

Where?	Touch Points	Customer Wants	Customer Action (Site Measures)	Customer Emotional Response & Why	Frequency x Impact on Customer Relationship	Root Cause		Improvement Suggestions
					1 1 3 5 5			
					1 1 3 5 5			
					1 1 3 5 5			
					1 1 3 5 5			
					1 1 3 5 5			
					1 1 3 5 5			

Recommendations

Customer Experience Worksheet

Improvement Suggestion Implementation Plan							
Improvement Suggestions							

6. Design Platform

Platform Map Introduction

"Value has moved from creating products and services to facilitating connections between external producers and consumers. The firm has collapsed as a center of production and instead has become the center of exchange. The areas where businesses could create and add economic value have shifted away from production and toward the curation and management of networks. That's where platform businesses come in."-- Modern Monopolies: What It Takes To Dominate in the 21st Century Economy", by Alex Moazed, Nicholas L. Johnsone

What does it mean to be a Platform?

Platform Map

Step 1: Describe the key components of the 3 Critical Layers.

	Community Layer	Infrastructure Layer	Data Layer
Components of Each Layer	Job-to-be-done (value created)	Services	Match supply with demand
	Vision	Business design/model/pricing	Match relevant content, goods and services to wants
	Core interactions	Partners	Processes and systems to provide deep insight into community
	Buyer and Supplier Profiles	Features and functionality	
	Buyer Value Proposition	Success Measures	
	Supplier Value Proposition:	Rules	
	Processes and systems to utilize deep insight provided by data layer	Tools	
	Community development strategy and tactics	Financial Model and Forecast	
	Community growth strategy and tactics		

Step 2: Fill in the Platform Canvas:

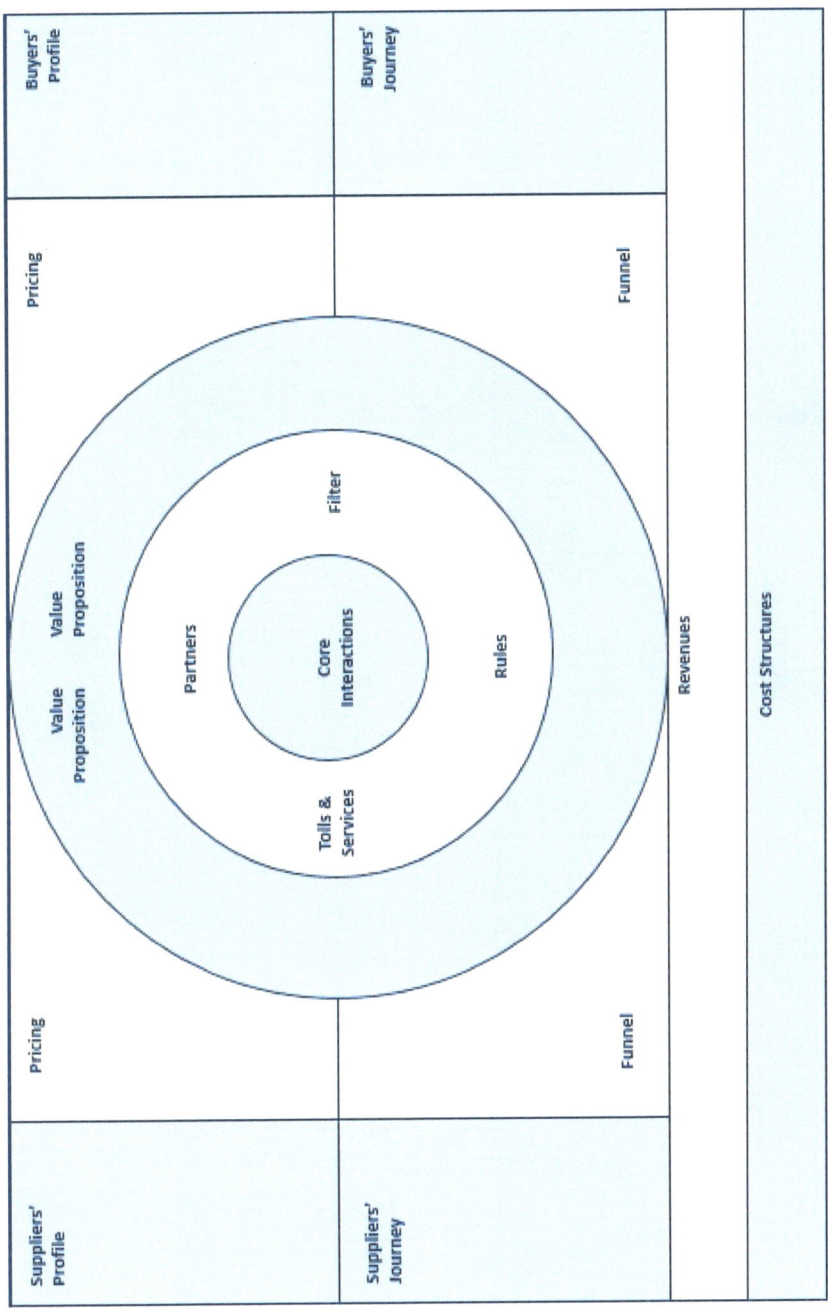

7. Prioritize Key Processes and Set Objectives

Your Business Model Canvas

Graphic representations of the key of variables necessary to scale an organization.

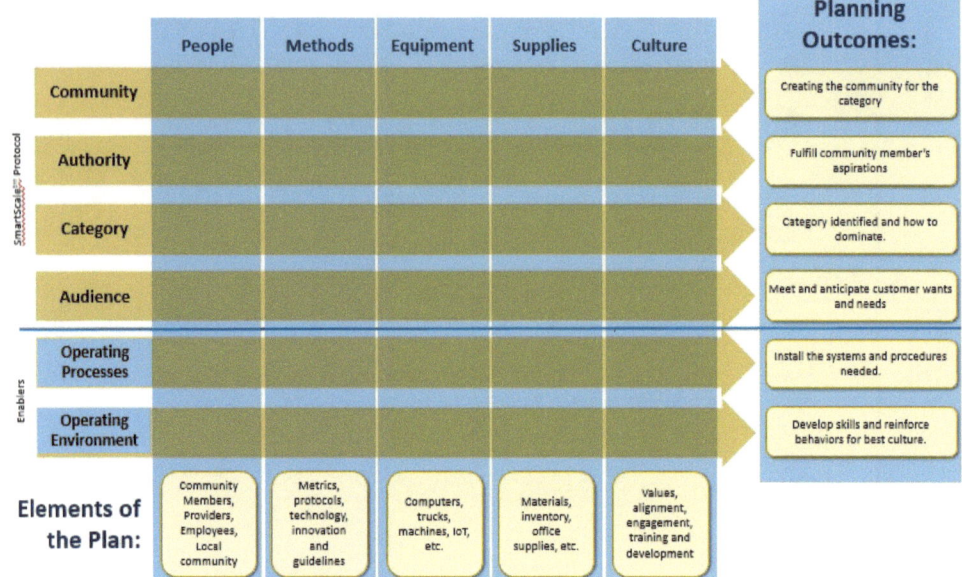

Your Scaling Canvas Action Plan

Action Steps	Responsibility	Deadline	Resources	Result
What task will be done?	Who will do it?	By when? (date)	What do you need to complete this step? (People, money, tools, processes, etc.)	What is the outcome of the task? (Measures)

The "Determine the Path to Scale" is designed to set your business up for scaling by:

1. Identifying opportunities to improve operations – thereby freeing up cash to reinvest in the scaling process.
2. Preparing business operations to accommodate scale.

This leadership initiative requires that key executives meet for two days away from the "day-to-day". It's an intense effort with evening breakout assignments.

Applying a "system thinking" construct, your team will quickly identify breakthrough changes and immediate improvement opportunities. You'll leave the sessions with:

- A strong sense of accountability for actively working with other leaders in improving the health of the company.
- A process map (Swimlane format) which visually depicts prioritized gaps needing leadership attention and closure.
- A game plan with realistic three-month financial benefits.
- Leadership's full endorsement and active support to execute the plan.
- Clear understanding of how the plan supports your SmartScale™ process.

8. Create Master Program of Projects

Master Plan for 5 - 8 Week Analysis and Planning Phase

	Key Milestones	Owner	Measurable Objectives	Resources	Start Date	Comp. Date	Notes
1							
2							
3							
4							
5							
6							
7							
7a							
7b							
7c							
8							
9							
10							

9. GoForward

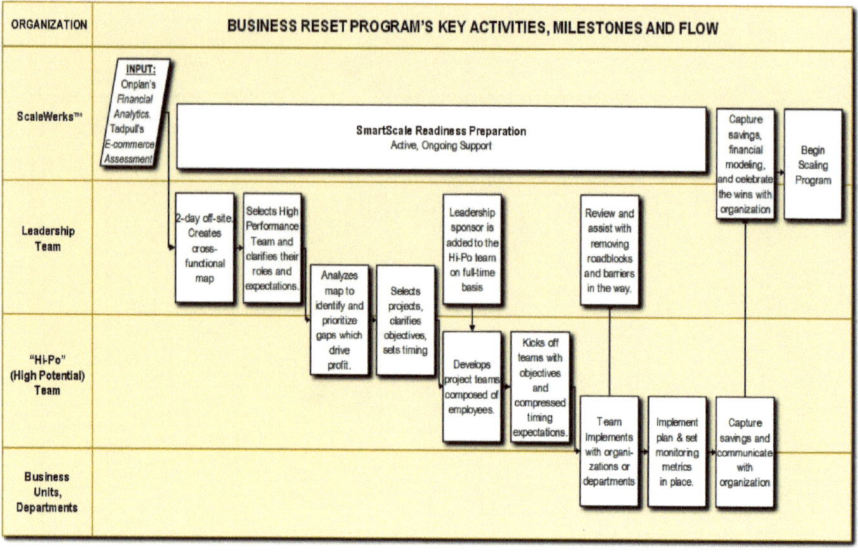

IMPLEMENT

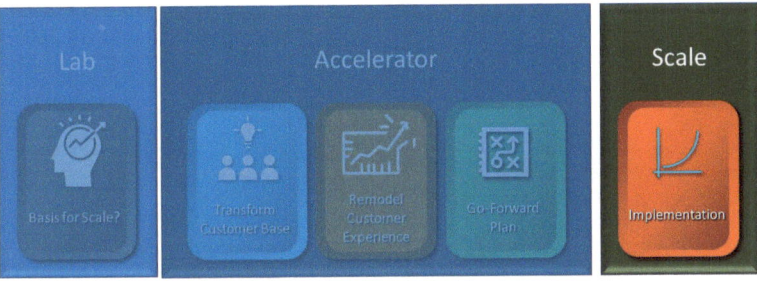

Tools and Methodologies

Process Map with "Swim Lanes"

We'll utilize "Swim lane" mapping in the 2-day offsite to help leadership see and understand, with common terms, how the company works *today*. The map is organized by employee, work group or department (in the swim lanes). Benefits include:

- Defines accountability
- Define work flows
- Identifies gaps
    - Unfulfilled needs during "hand-off's" (between departments or people)
    - Value-added time vs. time wasters
    - Rework
    - "Go Backs" for clarity, more information or rework.
    - Inspectors or checkers (review or check steps added to find mistakes)
- A design guide for architecting scale-ready operations

Symbol	What?	Requirements	Gap
Symbols most used for gap analysis			Difference between current vs. what it should be.
(hand-off figures)	Hand-off's from one department to another	100% on the *O-T-A-C scores	Can be a combination.
Delay	A waiting period or delay	How much time is allowed in the job specifications?	Impact downstream?
Process	Action or step	How does it add value? Can it be eliminated?	Do we need it?
In or Out	Something entering or leaving the process.	Based on customer / Supplier agreement	Achieve expectations?
Decision ?	Arrows show flow from "yes" or "no" decision.	100% on the *O-T-A-C scores	Needed? Made my right person(s)?
Valued 5m 9m 7m / Wasted 6m	Cycle Time Analysis	No wasted time.	Any wasted time.

Gap Analysis Using the Swim Lane Map

While creating the cross-functional map, we'll identify gaps that impact our ability to generate profit and revenue. The symbols we'll use and the gaps we'll be looking to close are:

Basic Symbols Used for Mapping

Symbol:	Start or End	Flow direction	Process	Document	Input / Output	Decision	Stored Data	More Paths
	Represents the start points, end points, and potential outcomes of a path. Often contains "Start" or "End" within the shape.	Connectors to all symbols used to show flow or work or information	Represents a process, action, or function. It's the most widely-used symbol in flowcharting	Represents the input or output of a document, specifically. Examples of and input are receiving a report, email, or order. Examples of an output using a document symbol include generating a presentation, memo, or letter.	Represents data that is available for input or output as well as representing resources used or generated.	Indicates a question to be answered — usually yes/no or true/false. The flowchart path may then split off into different branches depending on the answer or consequences thereafter.	This shape represents where data gets stored within a process.	This shape indicates that the process flow continues two paths or more.

The "Rules of the Road"

1) We do not "do it to you" and we do not do it "for you". We do it "with" you
2) Listen for the "voice of the customer" in everything we do
3) The words, "we've always done it that way" will never be spoken here
4) The leadership is open, and ready to drive change
5) Some decisions can only be made with "directional" data (avoid "data paralysis")
6) We want to hear ideas and concerns. Once a decision is made, we are all support it.
7) Less "I" - "my" - "mine" - "yours". More "we" and "ours"
8) No "sand bagging." We seldom exceed targets. Set aggressive, but achievable, targets.
9) Prevention is rewarded… crisis management represents "failure"

Immunity to Change

Change is hard, and even harder to maintain. Harvard Graduate School of Education professors Robert Kegan and Lisa Laskow Lahey posit that the challenge isn't a lack of willpower. Rather, they argue that failure to meet our goals may be the result of an emotional immune system that helps protect us from the fallout that can come from change—namely disappointment and shame.

In their book, Immunity to Change: How to Overcome It and Unlock the Potential in Yourself and Your Organization, Kegan and Lahey outline four critical steps for overcoming emotional pitfalls and arriving at true transformation.

To start, think about what's keeping you from your goal. What you perceive as obstacles could be competing commitments. Instead of surrendering your goal to a lack of time, money, or support, consider how you're utilizing these scarce resources.

Can you change the allocations? And, if so, will you be comfortable with the tradeoff? Is changing your leadership style worth the risk? Can you tolerate the professional reset you'll have to make by learning new skills?

When embracing change, you'll confront your core values and operating assumptions. Square off with the motivations that have been driving your decisions and determine whether those forces—such as stature, perfectionism, or risk aversion—are still relevant. If you are open to revising your guiding assumptions, you will find it easier to achieve your desired change.

If you are willing to work on these with your team, and you agree to work openly and authentically, with the understanding that it is safe (although demanding), you will dramatically increase the likelihood of success.

To uncover the issues that are inhibiting change and identify opportunities for improvement, Kegan and Lahey developed a four-step framework for tracking goals, overcoming perceived barriers, and outlining productive actions.

Immunity to Change Map & Instructions:

Improvement goal	Behaviors that work against my goal	Hidden competing commitments	Big assumptions
Step 1: Clear out obstructive behaviors	Step 2: Clear out obstructive behaviors	Step 3: Confront competing commitments	Step 4: Challenge your big assumptions
What's stalling your efforts? Maybe you find yourself crushed under a jam-packed schedule or consistently deprioritizing your goal in favor of more immediate tasks. Detail these behaviors in column two.	What's stalling your efforts? Maybe you find yourself crushed under a jam-packed schedule or consistently deprioritizing your goal in favor of more immediate tasks. Detail these behaviors in column two.	Here's where the real self-exploration comes in. Look at the behaviors you listed in column two and ask yourself how you'd feel if you did the opposite. Identify the fears you face in pursuing change by outlining key concerns in the box at the top of column three. Follow these concerns with what you fear will be compromised—your competing commitments.	In this last step, you'll identify the barriers you must overcome to achieve lasting change. Figure out what internalized truths are at the heart of your competing commitments by developing "if ____, then ____" statements. List these big assumptions in column four.
Gary wants to begin taking graduate Organizational Performance classes from an online institute, but working evenings and weekends (and juggling a personal life) has kept him from enrolling.	Gary wants to begin taking graduate Organizational Performance classes from an online institute, but working evenings and weekends (and juggling a personal life) has kept him from enrolling.	Gary worries that if he reduces his work schedule to make time for graduate courses, he'll be seen as slacker. And what if he finds that the coursework is too challenging? What if he invests the time and money to earn this credential, but then he realizes that he doesn't have the personality to be impactful? Gary's emotional immune system is clearly at work, warding off feelings of shame, disappointment, and fear before they can become real. By facing these feelings, Gary can begin to identify the commitments that are competing with his goal: seeking professional respect, performing at the highest level, and having security and stability.	For Gary, his big assumption might be "if I don't perform at the highest level, then I will be seen as a failure."

Immunity to Change Map & Worksheet

Improvement goal	Behaviors that work against my goal	Hidden competing commitments	Big assumptions
Actions to achieve my goal:		Worry box Competing commitments:	

Immunity to Change Map & Worksheet - TEAM

Our collective commitment	Doing/not doing instead	Our collective competing commitments	Our collective big assumptions
Actions to achieve our goal:		Worry box Competing commitments:	

Employee Engagement

Prosci's ADKAR model manages change with five phases of your employee's understanding:

Prosci Change Management Model

1. Awareness of need for change
2. Desire for making the change and supporting it

3. Knowledge on how to change
4. Reinforce the change once made

Managing change is vital for scaling because it:
- Drives buy-in through participation in the change
- Manages personal changes during the company-wide transition
- Focuses conversations about change
- Identifies actionable gaps
- Builds a measurement-driven, proactive culture

The purpose for ADKAR is to give each individual in the organization the knowledge and tools to actively support needed change.

Change Readiness Self Assessment

We have found the best way to understand the usefulness of the ADKAR model is to apply it to your own personal situation. Start by identifying a change you are having difficulty making in another person (a friend, family member, neighbor or work associate).

Complete the worksheet. Be sure to rate each element on a scale from 1, meaning no awareness to 5, meaning complete awareness. Select a change you have been dealing with but are having difficulty making.

Describe a personal change in behavior you are trying to make with a friend, family member, neighbor or work associate. Be brief.

		Answer these question:	Ranking instructions	Rank 1 - 5
A	A W A R E N E S S	List the reasons this change is required.	To what degree is person you are trying to change is aware of these reasons your wrote on the left? (Rank on a 1 to 5 scale, right)	
D	D E S I R E	List the factors or consequences (good and bad) for this person that would create a desire to change.	How well will these these motivating factors give the person a desire to change? (Rank on a 1 to 5 scale, right)	
K	K N O W L E D G E	List the skills and *knowledge* needed for the change, both during and after the transition.	Rate how aware this person is of the knowledge and skills you listed. (Rank on a 1 to 5 scale, right)	
A	A B I L I T Y	Consider the person's ability to perform or act in the new way. What barriers inhibit the person's ability?	How well equipped is this person abilities to implement the new skills, knowledge and behaviors. (Rank on a 1 to 5 scale, right)	
R	R E I N F O R C E	What will assure the change is permanent and not "slide back" to the old ways? Are incentives aligned?	How well are the reinforcements in place to support and maintain the change. (Rank on a 1 to 5 scale, right)	

Transfer your ranking scores from each ADKAR sections on previous page. Take a moment to review your scores. Highlight those areas that scored 3 or less – and identify which is the first area with a score of 3 or less. This first area will be your primary focus. Create a bar graph below showing your ADKAR change profile.

		Score from ranking sections
A	1. Awareness of the need to change	
D	2. Desire to make the change	
K	3. Knowledge about how to change	
A	4. Ability to change	
R	5. Reinforcement to maintain the change over time	

Now create an ADKAR profile bar graph. Mark your score for each element and shade the area below the mark to create each "bar." See example - a profile with A=4, D=5, K= 2, A=1, R=4.

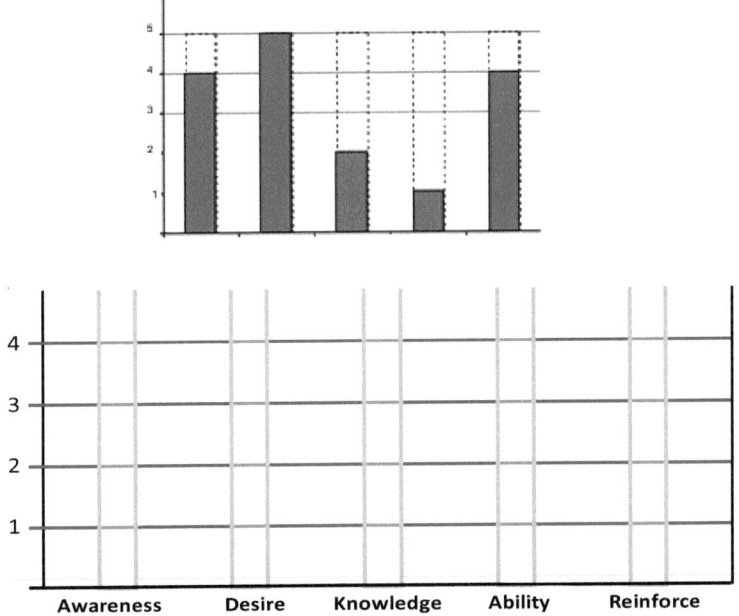

Organization Readiness Assessment for Significant Change Projects

*1=Strongly Disagree, 2=Disagree, 3=Neutral, 4= Somewhat Agree, 5=Agree 6=Strongly Agree

		Respond to each statement listed in the following five headings:	*Respond with 1–6
A		AWARENESS - Informing who is affected and impacted regarding this change. Respond to these questions below:	
	1	The organization has a clearly defined vision and strategy and changes are continually communicated with everyone in the organization.	
	2	Priorities are set and continually communicated regarding change projects and other competing initiatives.	
	3	The organization uses multiple communication methods to keep people informed.	
	4	The organization's messaging about change projects is clear, concise and consistent.	
	5	Mechanisms are in place to identify lapses in effective communication.	
A		Total AWARENESS Score / 5 = Average Score	
B		LEADERSHIP - Ensuring there is active leadership sponsoring the change is important. Respond to these questions below:	
	6	Change initiatives within the organization have an executive assigned to sponsor and support the change.	
	7	The executive sponsor has the necessary authority over the people, processes and systems to authorize and fund change initiatives.	
	8	The executive sponsor has the capabilities to build organization-wide awareness of the need for change. (why the change is happening).	
	9	The executive sponsor will actively and visibly participate with the project team throughout the entire change process.	
	10	The executive sponsor will resolve issues and make decisions relating to the change project schedule, scope and resources.	
B		Total LEADERSHIP Score / 5 =Average Score	
C		DESIRE - Gaining buy-in for the changes from those involved and affected, directly or indirectly is important. Respond to these questions below:	
	11	The executive sponsor is willing and able to build a sponsorship coalition for change and is able to manage resistance from all stakeholders.	
	12	Change successes are celebrated, at all levels of the organization.	
	13	People hear a consistent and unified message from all levels of management with executives leading the way.	
	14	Change initiatives are accurately tailored to the particular needs and concerns of each employee or groups.	
	15	Special tactics have been developed for handling opposition to change from any one or group in the organization.	
C		Total DESIRE Score / 5 = Average Score	

Readiness Assessment Continued

	Respond to each statement listed in the following five headings:	*Respond with 1–6
D	INFRASTRUCTURE – Having a good structure in place and a discipline planning process is important. Respond to these questions below:	
16	A structured change management approach is being communicated and applied to change projects.	
17	Change management team members have been identified. Managers and staff are trained on how to effectively manage change.	
18	Project teams are tracking progress and able to resolve related issues through set project management processes. Change management plans are integrated into all projects involving people.	
19	Any resources need for change projects are identified and acquired.	
20	Feedback processes are continually used to determine how effectively change is being adopted by everyone in the organization.	
D	Total INFRASTRUCTURE Score / 5 = Average Score	
E	KNOWLEDGE - Training the appropriate resources on the change. Respond to these questions below:	
21	Organization recognizes and reinforces skills and behaviors required for the change effort.	
22	Skills and knowledge needed for transition have been identified.	
23	Skills are continually identified for conducting change projects.	
24	Training is developed and scheduled proactively, based on gaps and need assessments.	
25	Training to very assessable to all employees in various venues (classroom, web-based, video, etc.)	
E	Total KNOWLEDGE Score / 5 = Average Score	

For a visual of the results, draw columns in the graph below. Anything below a "4" should be addressed.

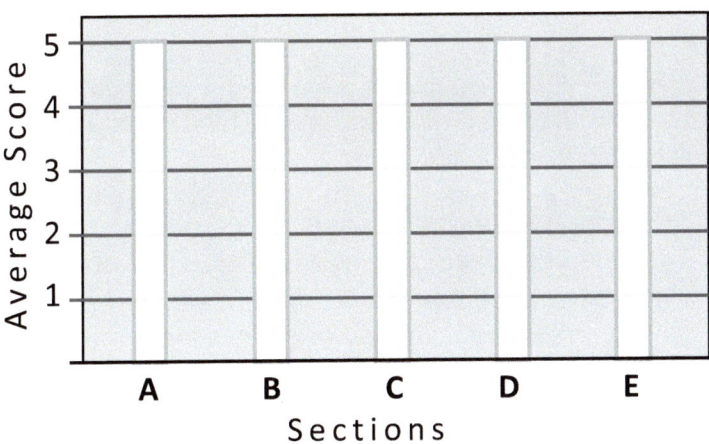

Glossary

SmartScale™ – A technical and adaptive process for scaling mid-life companies.

ScaleWerks™ Business Model Canvas – A visual chart that provides a high level illustration of the SmartScale™ Protocol.

Core Protocols – The key dimensions of the SmartScale™ Business Model Canvas: Audience, Category, Authority and Community.

- **Audience:** Prospects and customers that have interest in learning more about or hiring a business to do a specific job.
- **Category:** A market niche that is defined by how the job a company does satisfies customer wants.
- **Authority:** The position a company earns in the minds of its prospects and customers for deep knowledge, expertise and capability to accomplish the job that customers want to have the company do for them.
- **Community:** The category-centric environment where customers interact (connect and collaborate) with the authority – and recognize the authority as the Category Leader.

Enablers – Underlying technical capabilities and adaptive skills to support the SmartScale™ process categorized as Operating Environment and Operating Processes

- **Operating Environment:** Cultural drivers and adaptive skills that drive Category Leadership and Scale.
- **Operating Processes:** Technology, systems and procedures that drive Category Leadership and Scale.

Category Leader: The recognized authority and community leader in a category (category defined as a market niche that is defined by how the job a company satisfies customer wants).

ScaleWerks™ Scaling Implementation Canvas – A visual chart used as an introduction to the SmartScale™ Analysis and Plan Design.

Systems Thinking: a holistic approach to analysis that focuses on the way that a system's constituent parts interrelate and how systems work over time and within the context of larger systems.

Bibliography

The Expertise Economy: How the Smartest Companies Use Learning To Engage, Compete, And Succeed
Palmer & Blake - Nicholas Brealey Publishing – 2018

Immunity to Change How to Overcome It and Unlock the Potential in Yourself and Your Organization
Kegan et al. - Harvard Business Review Press – 2009

Modern Monopolies: What It Takes To Dominate the 21st-Century Economy
Moazed & Johnson - St. Martin's Press – 2016

Platform Scale: How an Emerging Business Model Helps Startups Build Large Empires with Minimum Investment
Choudary - Platform Thinking Labs Pte. Ltd. – 2015

Disrupt: Think the Unthinkable To Spark Transformation in Your Business
Williams - Financial Times/Prentice Hall – 2015

What's Your Digital Business Model? Six Questions to Help You Build the Next-Generation Enterprise
Weill & Woerner - Harvard Business Review Press – 2018

What Would Google Do? Reverse Engineering the Fastest Growing Company in the History of the World
Jarvis - HarperPaperbacks – 2011

Become a Key Person of Influence
Priestley - Ecademy Press – 2010

Measure What Matters: Online Tools for Understanding Customers, Social Media, Engagement, and Key Relationships
Paine & Paarlberg - Wiley – 2011

Exponential Organizations: Why New Organizations Are Ten Times Better, Faster, and Cheaper Than Yours (And What to Do About It)
Ismail et al. - Diversion Books – 2014

Platform Revolution: How Networked Markets Are Transforming the Economy and How To Make Them Work For You
Parker et al. - W. W. Norton & Company – 2017

Platform Strategy: How to Unlock the Power of Communities and Networks to Grow Your Business
Reillier & Reillier - Routledge, Taylor & Francis Group – 2017

Digital @ Scale: How You Can Lead Your Business to the Future with Digital@Scale
Swaminathan & Meffert - Wiley – 2017

Strategy beyond the Hockey Stick: People, Probabilities, and Moves to Beat the Odds
Bradley et al. - Wiley – 2018

The Three Box Solution: A Strategy for Leading Innovation
Govindarajan - Harvard Business Review Press – 2016

Virus of the Mind: The New Science of the Meme
Brodie - Hay House – 2011

Jobs to Be Done: A Roadmap for Customer-Centered Innovation
Wunker et al. - AMACOM – 2017

The Art of Community: Building the New Age of Participation
Bacon - O'Reilly & Associates – 2012

Social Selling: Techniques To Influence Buyers And Changemakers
Hughes & Reynolds - Kogan Page – 2016

YouthNation: Building Remarkable Brands in a Youth-Driven Culture
Britton - John Wiley & Sons – 2015

Blitzscaling: the lightning-fast path to building massively valuable businesses
Hoffman & Yeh - Currency - 2018

www.ingramcontent.com/pod-product-compliance
Lightning Source LLC
Chambersburg PA
CBHW040322220526

45473CB00009B/2539